Sweet Dreams, Sarah

By Vivian Kirkfield
Illustrated by Chris Ewald

Creston Books

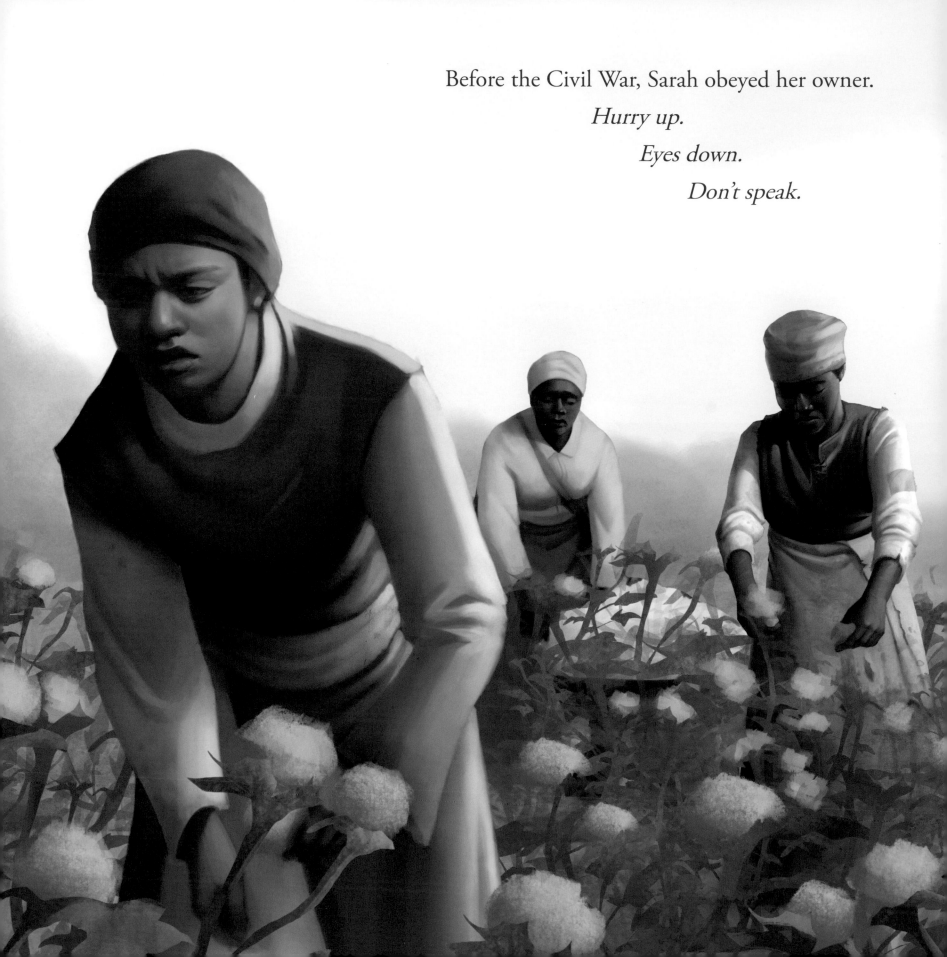

Before the Civil War, Sarah obeyed her owner.

Hurry up.

Eyes down.

Don't speak.

Slaves were property — like a cow or plow or the cotton that grew in the master's fields.

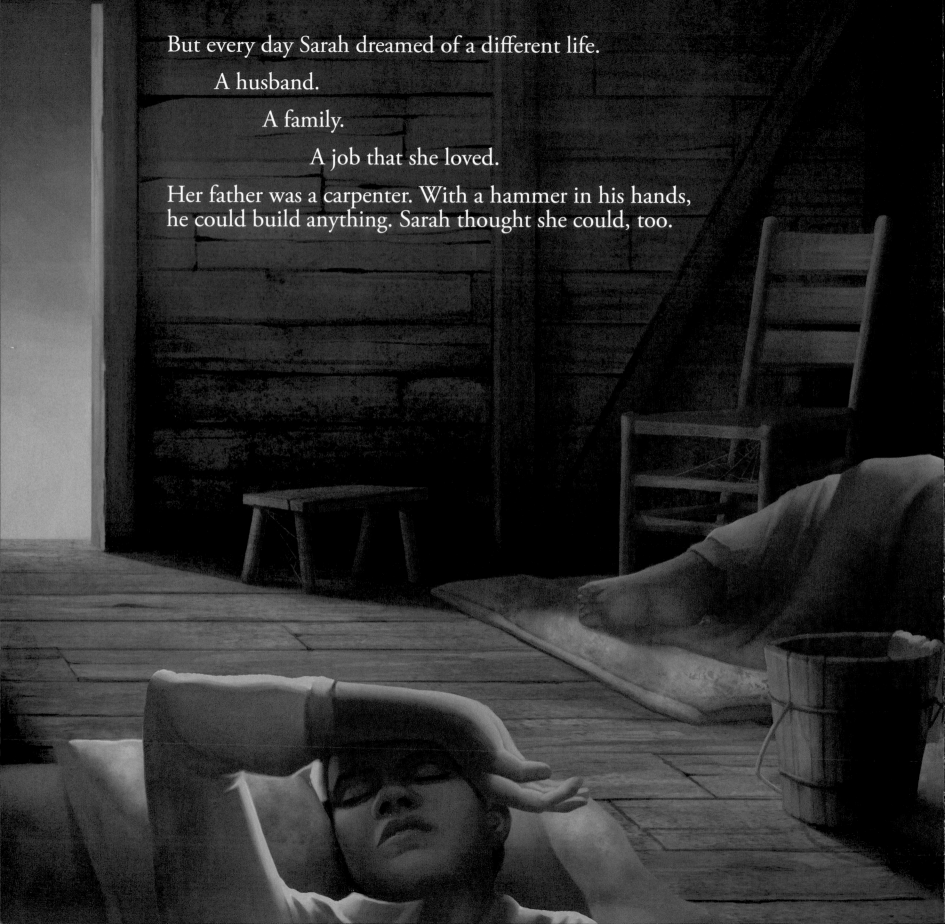

But every day Sarah dreamed of a different life.

A husband.

A family.

A job that she loved.

Her father was a carpenter. With a hammer in his hands,
he could build anything. Sarah thought she could, too.

Then something happened that changed their lives forever.
A new law freed people from slavery.

Sarah moved to Chicago with

freedom in her pocket,

hope in her heart,

and dreams swirling in her head.

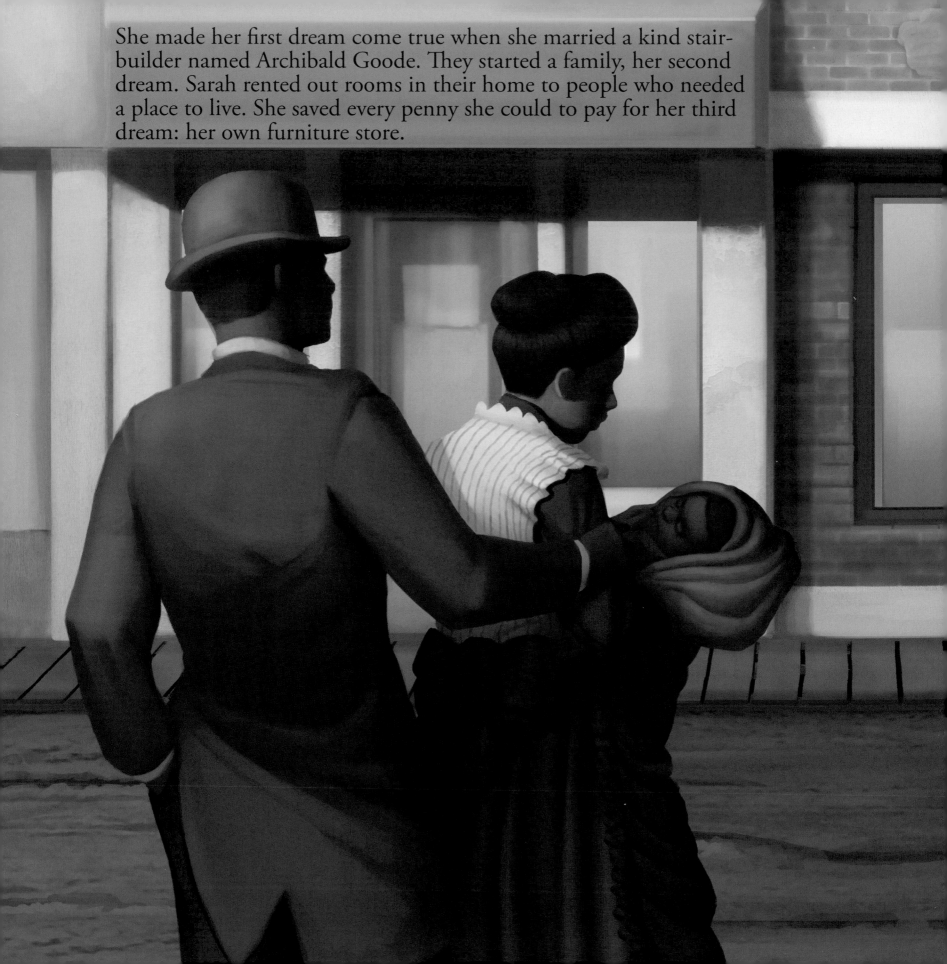

She made her first dream come true when she married a kind stair-builder named Archibald Goode. They started a family, her second dream. Sarah rented out rooms in their home to people who needed a place to live. She saved every penny she could to pay for her third dream: her own furniture store.

Every day Sarah worked alongside her husband.

Measure.

Cut.

Sand.

And every day Sarah
listened to her customers.

Pretty crowded at our place.

*There are five of us crammed
into one room.*

Sure wish the kids had their own bed.

Many of Sarah's customers worked at low-paying jobs. And even those with big families could only afford to live in a one-room apartment.

Sarah looked at the furniture in their store.

Too boxy!

Too bulky!

Too big!

Then Sarah had an idea, another dream. Maybe she could build a piece of furniture that would save space for her customers.

If she could create a new kind of bed that folded up when it wasn't being used, each kid could have their own bed.

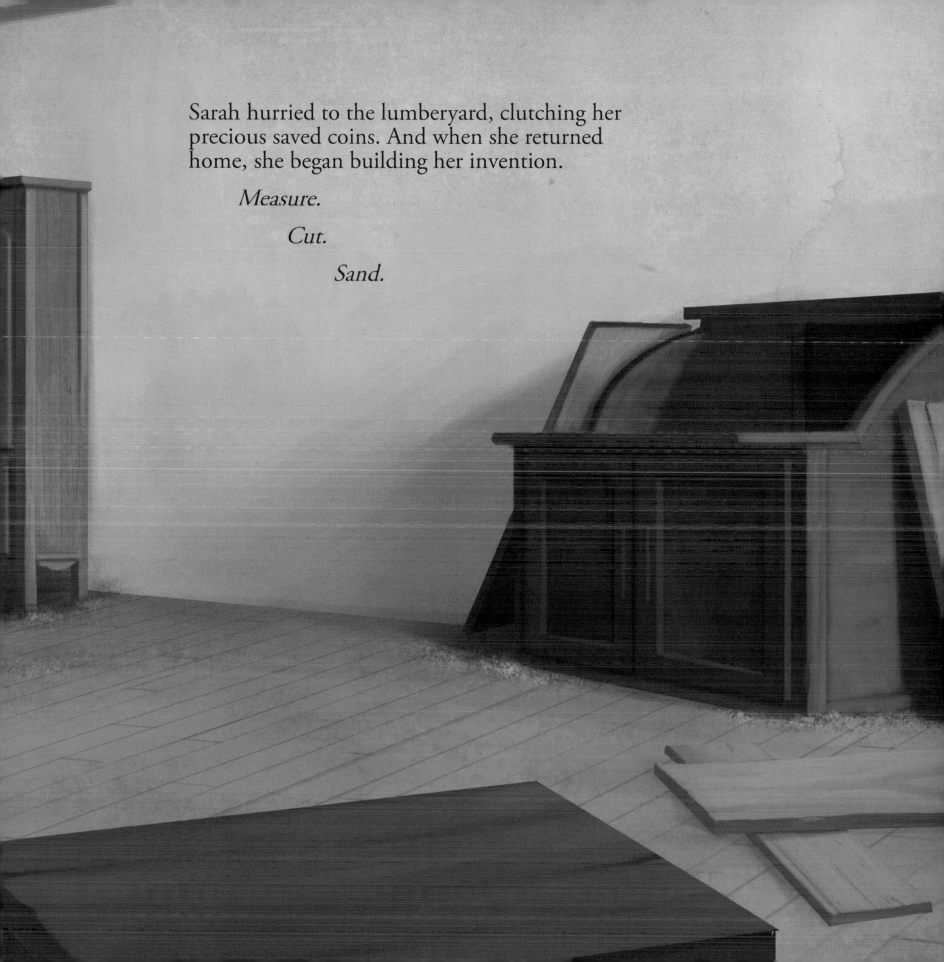

Sarah hurried to the lumberyard, clutching her precious saved coins. And when she returned home, she began building her invention.

Measure.

Cut.

Sand.

Finally, she hammered in the last nail. Standing back, she looked at her creation — a desk — but not just any desk. Inside the cabinet doors, a fold-out bed was hidden.

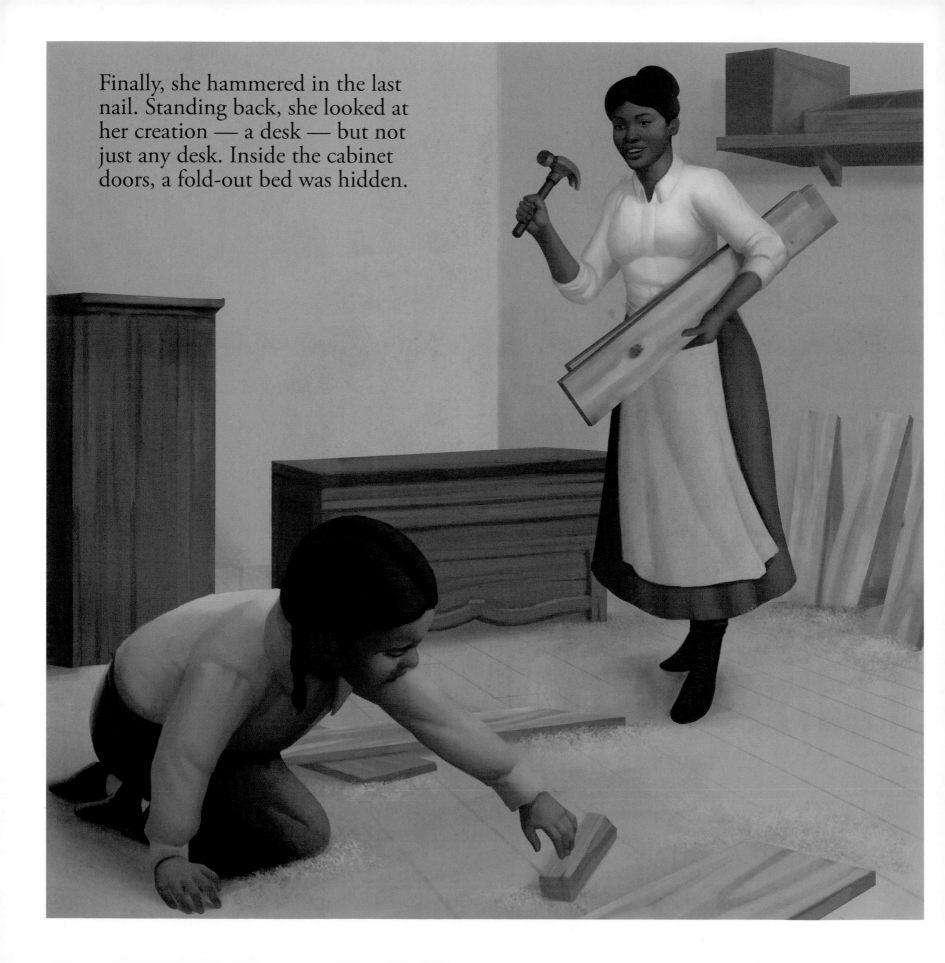

Sarah pulled. She pushed.

STUCK!

Sarah took it all apart and started over again. But everything went wrong.

Wood split.

Nails bent.

The bed wouldn't lay flat.

Sarah didn't give up. She took a deep breath and dove right in to fix it. Again.

At last she stepped back and smiled. Now, when she pulled out the bed, it slid back in without a catch or a squeak. Archibald wanted to sell it in the store right away, but Sarah knew there was one more thing she had to do.

She'd dreamt it.

She'd built it.

Now she needed to claim it.

Sarah needed to get a patent. A patent is a piece of paper from the government that says no one else can make or sell your invention. If someone else got the patent first, Sarah would lose the right to make and sell her cabinet beds.

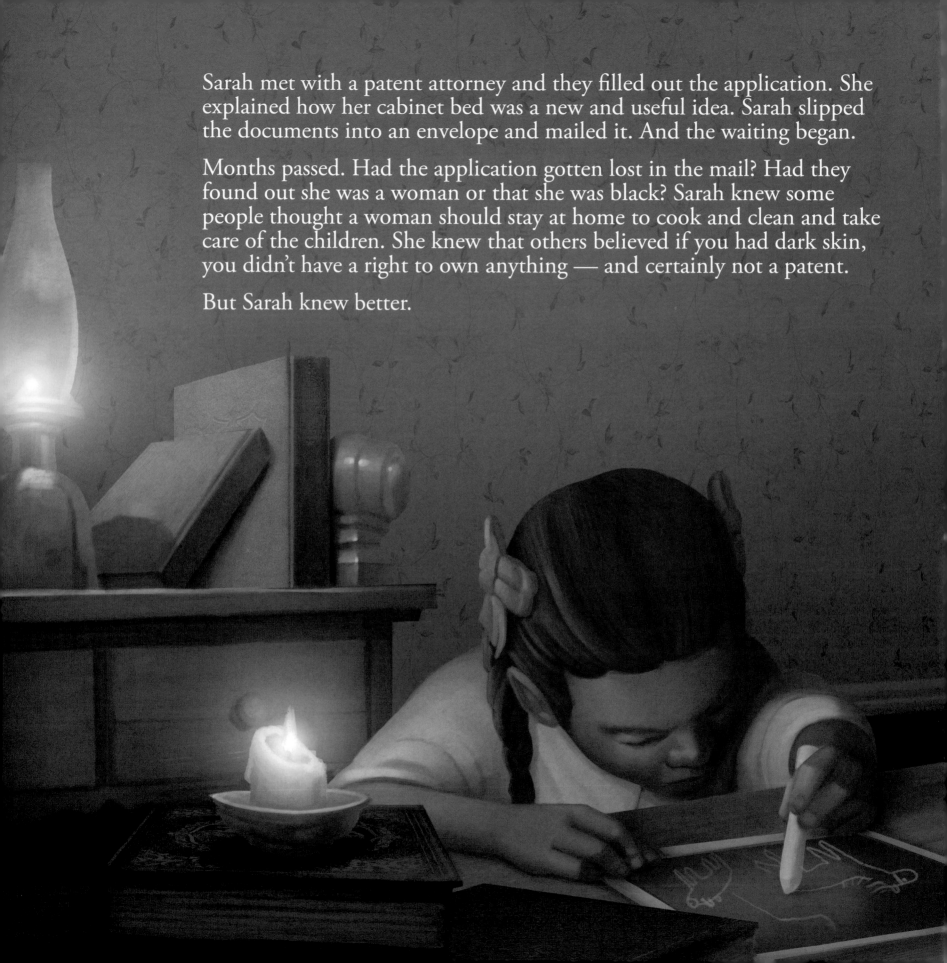

Sarah met with a patent attorney and they filled out the application. She explained how her cabinet bed was a new and useful idea. Sarah slipped the documents into an envelope and mailed it. And the waiting began.

Months passed. Had the application gotten lost in the mail? Had they found out she was a woman or that she was black? Sarah knew some people thought a woman should stay at home to cook and clean and take care of the children. She knew that others believed if you had dark skin, you didn't have a right to own anything — and certainly not a patent.

But Sarah knew better.

After a year, a letter finally arrived.

DENIED

There were already patents on similar inventions.
Sarah needed to prove hers was different.

Carefully she changed a word here and a sentence there, explaining more about her unique mechanism, the idea that had come to her so long ago. Slipping the paperwork and a bit of her heart into the envelope, Sarah sealed her fate and sent it off. Once again, she waited.

This time a thick envelope arrived from the U.S. Government Patent Office.

Sarah took a slow deep breath.

She slid out the papers.

She read out loud:

S. E. GOODE.
CABINET BED.
No. 322,177. Patented July 14, 1885.

Staring at her name in print, Sarah proudly traced each letter. Her idea, her invention, her name in history. She had built more than a piece of furniture. She had built a life far away from slavery, a life where her sweet dreams could come true.

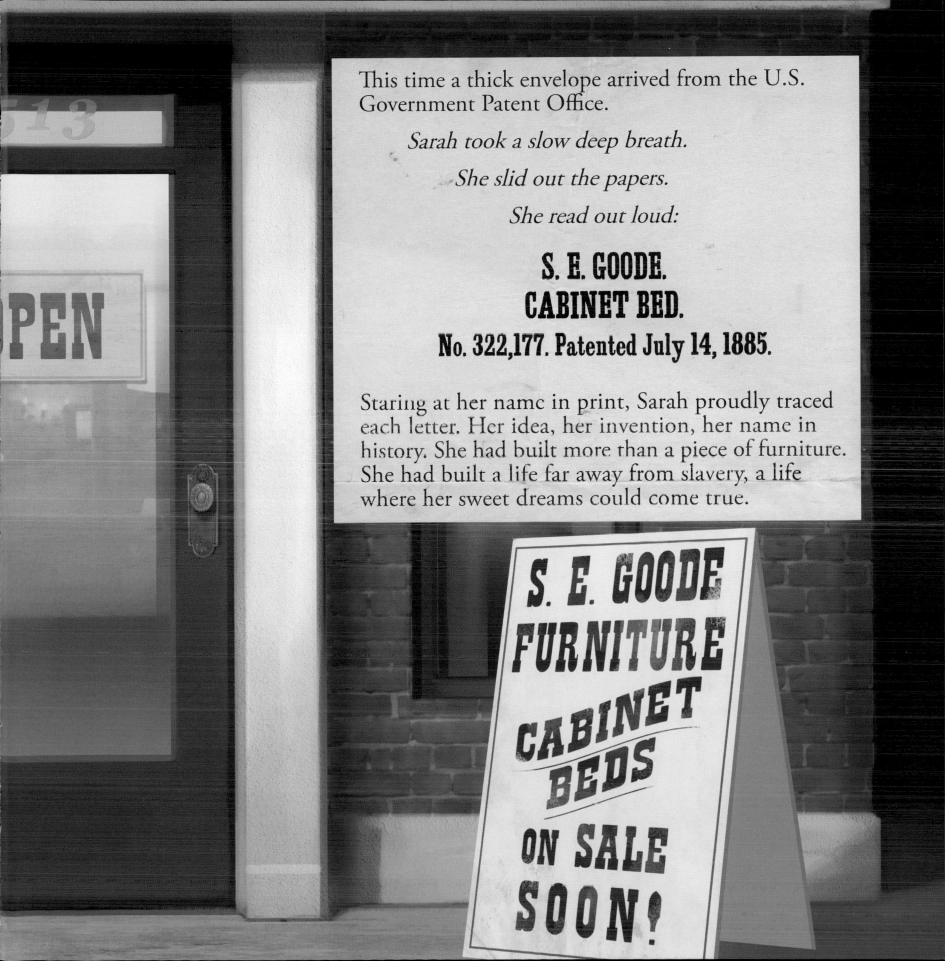

Author's Note

Many of the details of Sarah's life are not known. What we do know is that by 1870, Sarah and her family were living in Chicago. According to the census, Sarah's father, a skilled carpenter, had real estate worth $10,000 and personal assets worth $3000. In today's dollars, his property would be worth over $150,000—an extraordinary achievement for a black man only five years after the end of the Civil War. When Sarah was ready to start her own business, her parents may have helped her financially, as many parents do these days for their children.

In both the North and the South, African American men and women were treated like second class citizens. Job opportunities were limited. Housing choices were restricted. But Sarah E. Goode refused to give up her dream. She opened her furniture store at a time when women could not even vote or own property and she made her place in history with her patent for the cabinet bed, pushing open the door for those who would come after her.

The cabinet bed became extremely popular because it allowed people to save space. Sarah's invention inspired other similar innovations in furniture. The Murphy bed, which folded up into a closet, was created in 1916. Today all over the world, in homes, hotels, and businesses, millions of fold-away beds are in use. Have you ever slept on a fold-up bed?

What is a Patent?

A patent is a right granted by the government. It is a legal document issued to protect an idea. It says that other people cannot make or sell your invention. What is granted is not the right to make or use or sell the invention, but the right to prevent others from making, using, or selling the invention.

There are three types of patents. **Utility patents** are granted to anyone who invents or discovers any new and useful process, machine, or article of manufacture or any new and useful improvement of those. **Design patents** are for new, original, and ornamental designs for an existing product or process. **Plant patents** are granted for any distinct and new variety of plant.

For more information on patents: www.uspto.gov/kids

Sarah E. Goode Timeline

1856: Sarah Elisabeth Jacobs is born. Some sources say she was born in the south, others say Ohio. If you look at the map, the southern border of Ohio runs along Virginia's northern one. Her father was a freedman. Her mother was a slave. It might have made sense for her family to claim their children were born in the free state of Ohio, instead of the slave state of Virginia.

1863: Emancipation Proclamation – President Abraham Lincoln abolishes slavery.

1865: Civil War ends and African Americans form a great migration, heading north, many to big cities like Chicago to find jobs.

1870: Chicago census shows Sarah is age 15, attending school and living with her father, Oliver, her mother, Harriet, and her siblings, Oliver, Hattie, and Lincoln.

1870: The 15th Amendment to the Constitution grants African American men the right to vote but does not grant suffrage to women, whether white or black.

1880: Chicago census shows Sarah is age 24, married to Archibald Goode, a stair builder. Sharing their home are her brother-in-law, Robert, her two-year old daughter, Inez, and four lodgers.

1883: On November 12th, Sarah pays a $15 fee and mails her application for the cabinet bed (with drawings and lengthy explanations for each of the moving parts). George P. Barton of 99 Randolph Street, Chicago serves as her patent attorney.

1884: Application is denied because some of the parts of the cabinet bed had already been patented by others. Sarah, with the help of her attorney, rewords the application and mails it back.

1884: An advertisement in the Cleveland Gazette shows S.E. Goode, Prop. of two furniture store locations – one at 513 State Street and one at 2110 Wabash Avenue, both in Chicago.

1885: On July 14th, Sarah's patent is approved.

1886: Sarah E. Goode appears in Chicago's city listing and business listing (under Furniture).

1887: An advertisement in the Chicago Daily Inter-Ocean newspaper on May 4th shows a cabinet bed for sale. The copy reads: "manufacturer of these beds went bust and we are now the exclusive distributors." We may never know why Sarah and her husband lost their business – illness, bad luck, or jealousy and possibly violence from business competitors – but there is one thing Sarah will never lose: her place in history. Sarah E. Goode will always be one of the first African American women in U.S. history to be recorded as earning a patent for her invention.

1905: On April 4th, Sarah E. Goode dies at age 49 and is buried in Graceland Cemetery in Chicago, Illinois.

Timeline of Black Women Patent Holders

1883: Sarah E. Goode applies for cabinet bed patent that is issued in 1885.

1884: Judy Reed – Improvement to dough kneader and roller

1888: Miriam Benjamin – Gong and signal chairs for hotels

1892: Sarah Boone – Ironing board

1892: Anna Mangin – Pastry fork

1896: Julia Terry Hammonds – Apparatus for holding yarn skeins

1898: Lyda Newman – Hair brush

1903: Mary Anderson – Windshield wipers

1905: Madame C.J. Walker – Hair care products with straightening comb

1907: Clara Frye – Surgical appliance

1905: Madeline Turner – Fruit press

1919: Alice Parker – Heating furnace

1920: Mary Toland – Float-operated circuit closer

1920: Mary Jane Reynolds – Hoisting and loading mechanism

1928: Marjorie Joyner – Permanent hair waving machine

1929: Virginia Scharschmidt – Safety window cleaning device

1935: Margaret Cheetham – Interactive toy with cat chasing rat

1937: Marry and Harry Jackson – Burglar alarm

1943: Henrietta Bradberry – Bed rack attachment for airing out clothes

1945: Henrietta Bradberry – Torpedo discharger

1946: Jessie T. Pope – Croquignole iron for hair

1950: Lydia Holmes – Easy-to-assemble wooden wheeled toys

1951: Bessie Blount Griffin – Device to help disabled feed themselves

1956: Beatrice Kenner – Sanitary belt

1959: Bertha Berman – Fitted bedsheets

1960: Iula O. Carter – Nursery chair

1960: Jessie May Pope – Hair conditioning implement

1969: Marie Van Brittan Brown – Home security system utilizing TV surveillance

1973: Gertrude Downing (with William Desjardin) – Corner cleaning attachment for rotary floor treatment machine (she got several subsequent patents for improvements)

1976: Virgie Ammons – Fireplace damper

1976: Mary Beatrice Kenner – Carrier attachment for walker

1977: Virginia Hall and Beatrice Cowans (co-inventors) – Embroidered fruit bowl wall hanging and kit to make it

1978: Debrilla Ratchford – Suitcase with wheels and transporting hook

1980: Valerie Thomas – Illusion transmitter

1980: Mildred Smith – Family relationship card game

1981: Carol Randel – Ear clips

1981: Brothella Quick – Pocketed underwear

1983: Theora Stephens – Pressing/curling iron

1983: Maxine Snowden – Rain hat

1985: June Horne – Emergency escape apparatus

1986: Betty Harris – Color-spot test to determine the presence of TATB, an explosive

1987: Joan Clark – Medicine tray

1987: Ruane Jeter – Digital toaster

1988: Patricia Bath – Apparatus for removing cataracts

1990: Dawn Francis – Organic fertilizer

1991: Sharon Barnes – Device that measures temperature of urine sample without touching it

1992: Wanda Sigur – Fabrication of high strength-low weight laminated structures of unlimited size

1992: Natalie Love – Removable cover for T-top convertible cars

1993: Joanna Hardin – Keyboard stand

1994: Tanya Allen – Disposable underwear

1999: Joycelyn Harrison – Membrane tension control and a dozen other patents including a 2018 patent for a polymer solar panel that provides better shielding

2000: Ruth Miro – Improved metal rings to hold a sheaf of papers together

2004: Ruth Miro – Stationery organizer

2006: Janet Bashen – Web-based software program for Equal Employment Opportunity claims and report management